Guest of Time

First Lieutenant Greg in the field, Vietnam, 1969

Also by Greg McBride
Porthole

Guest of Time

A Memoir in Poems
Greg McBride

POND ROAD PRESS
NORTH TRURO, MASSACHUSETTS

ISBN: 978-1-7336574-2-6

Library of Congress Control Number: 2023937305

Pond Road Press
P.O. Box 30
North Truro, Massachusetts 02652-0030
pondroadpress@hotmail.com

Printed in the United States of America.

10 9 8 7 6 5 4 3 2 1

for Lois, Rhondda, and Kerry,
Bake, Berle, Bill, Dan, David, Don, Dubs,
Gigi, Goose, Gordie, Hailey, Marty, Terence
George, Nels, and Will
and the Capitol Hill Poetry Group

The imposed life at odds
with the soul's discoveries
—Heraclitus

Contents

Making

Notes

Acknowledgments

Bio

Making

The way the warm
rainwater beads
on the bent leaf

gathers tension
swells in heft
glitters   suspends

drops
to something less
than itself

something lost
an orb no more
at some cost

contour   scope
yet feeding
another something

something more
than this world knew
moments before.

Guest of Time

Bitterroot

*Can a father give his son
what he himself never possessed,
or lacks the courage to wish up
from his own deprivation?*
—Galway Kinnell

The wind poured down Bitterroot Range
sprinkling a cloak of white across the flatland
ironed out to the far horizon where the edge
of that big blue sky opened to receive
the upward thrust of trees and boys
who fed on Idaho's high, white light,
just as Shoshone boys ran the land,
the land of their fathers, till came
the Oregon Trail and Massacre Rocks.
Great cumuli gathered and reared, stately
in their drift onward toward the Great Plains.
Clopping sorrels flicked black tails against
the horse-fly storms, startled at the roar
and spew of Model T's. My father and his brothers
ran the shallows near the falls where the river
began its arc, and fields furrowed deep to black,
dirt roads rutted through spring grass.

In 1878, my father's father, Sören,
was born to a Danish mother who spoke
no English. He married Eliza,
a sail maker's daughter from Yorkshire,
my father one of her bairns, one of her many.
He was five when the town abandoned
American Falls and rebuilt on higher ground,
leaving every home and shop and general store
submerged for the new Snake River dam.
Sören worked as its foreman for fifty years,

their small company house perched out over the river.
On a clear day, they could peer into the deep
below, the corner market, the pathways,
their old home. All the places wavered up
to them through the ceaseless current.

My father alone survived boyhood.
Richard climbed onto the iceman's turning
wagon wheel; it snapped his neck. Merlin
was crushed beneath a falling horse,
my father, four, watching from the wagon bench.
Another died in infancy, another
a miscarriage. Sören's grief so crushing
he could not father my father. My father
never spoke his brothers' names, never spoke
of his father. Standing at his coffin,
I leaned over where he lay, proud
in his shiny dress blues, and kissed
his still-smooth forehead, cold and hard.

Vintage Photograph
at Sea

I teeter at the curve
of her hip and tuck
the soft-blond top

of my head well below
her cloth-coated arm,
a white milk truck

missing a wheel clutched
to my chest, cold wind
whipping sea spray

across the lurching deck
in '48. First mate
in my mother's navy,

all's well it seems to me.
Without a fight,
in my mother's care,

I will occupy Japan.
We will be content
while black and white.

Portland

I.

When others speak of their hometowns, I think
of what we had of home and town, Portland
foremost of the dozens we would have,
I then five, you just three, the year we moved
to Winchell Street, the tiny house sitting
on a rise, like a frosted birthday cake.
That first day, we dashed around the yard,
our parents exhausted. We ripped lush leaves
from the profusion that is Portland,
the price: play-paying in veined greenbacks.
It was a movie-heaven to me then
—1950—our father, just thirty,
tossing us into the blue. There would be
treasure in the alleys, precious stones,
arrowheads, the detritus of feathered
hunters camped nearby, not so long before,
I was sure. The gang we ran with
thought us twins—I was so small—and I
wondered, could we be twins by wishing it
enough? You, a little girl made of something
big, seized each day with fierce intent. And I,
I wanted to stand out, whether up or down,
to leave my mark once we drifted on again.

II.

Back in Portland fifty-odd years later,
I returned to Winchell, almost on a whim.
Smaller than I recalled, the house slumped
on its small hill, wan from the wear
of generations, in vacant disrepair,
the roses overtaken, the street ill-kempt.
Hooding my eyes, I peered through the dust-
encrusted windows where our 25-year-old

mother made peanut butter sandwiches
and poured us milk. I knelt to my knees,
inhaled the earthy grass, fondled the soil
she worked in kitchen gloves, her table fork
digging space for angel wing begonias.

III.

Yielding to the part of myself that weeps
in the dark of sentimental movies,
I rolled onto the back of my blue-grey suit,
the trees high against the same sere-blue sky.
I wanted to breathe, to taste, Portland air,
to wrap myself around our past—longing
for our young parents, for you, for my own
past self, for those years of passing through
pastel and neon motels, troopships, prop planes,
Quonset huts, through open-heart attachments
then detachments then diversions of the road:
—Abilene to Carthage, San Diego—
—Utah, Baltimore, to Philadelphia—
my Sal Maglie glove giving off the sweet scent
of kipskin leather and neatsfoot oil
—Yokohama, Arizona, Oregon—
the Philco shouting the joy of Don Larsen's
perfect game, crackling the news: Einstein died.

IV.

When one of us is gone, our Portland
will teeter on the edge of effacement,
and the other will fall in line, in place,
marching among other ordinaries
along Winchell Street, one block to the next.
Meanwhile, I'm collecting these past selves
and of these bits constructing another
momentary self, not so much to leave
a mark as to spit in the eye of extinction.

The Cosmologist

It was dark. I was ten. I could not sleep.
Space and endlessness and immensity
got in my way. What could it mean?

She was always worried, my mom.
She cracked the door. A thin stream
of light knifed in onto the floor.

She sat on the edge of my bed.
Her hand cupped my cheek. We're lost
in the dark of a great somewhere.

It's a nightmare, she said.

Whistling

We lived in a Victorian a block
from Muscle Beach the year my dad was stationed
in Okinawa. My cousin's family too.
A family friend would whistle hello
when he drove up out front. He taught me
to whistle too. Maybe his name was Jack.
We played Monopoly—I got the top hat.
He was a nice man with wavy hair
like my dad's. Maybe his name was Bob.
One day we packed my T-shirts and sleepers,
my ball and jacks and pogo stick, and flew
the Pacific to my dad. Someone said
the nice man died; still, he traveled with me
through that year, and many more, until
his name, then his face, blurred into the muddle
of my grandfather's graveled voice, the warmth
of my mother's scent. My cousin says it was
five blocks to the beach. My sister says the house
was a bungalow and neat. They both say
there was no Jack, or Bob, in those days.
Before she died, my aunt said the same.
Fingers angled just so, I still whistle his way.

The Table

Ten bucks at the Old Stuff Shop.
All of us together then
on the kitchen floor, our captain
father disassembling top from base,
base from splayed claw feet.
They fixed and stripped week by week,
our mother cross-legged on the tile,
rootling toothpicks at the crannies.
The squawk and skreegh of aged oak
accented our father's hums and cusses
until, with rising satisfaction,
he began to whistle *Begin*
the Beguine. He reassembled,
made it tight, and the metronomic
rasp of his sander unearthed
a wash of woody forest scent
from the flesh of fresh-cut trees.
I could not get enough of it,
all of us together then
around the salvaged table.

Counting Marbles

On a Portland playground,
scalawags with limber wrists,
we knelt at stick-drawn rings in dirt,
then anted-up—and thereby risked—

agates, clay-fired taws, hard-won
thumbings of rapt summer boys
who ignored the tetherball,
baseball, the diving board noise.

Midas at ten, I swaggered home,
pockets bulged with winnings,
and filled another coffee tin
for Sunday morning counting.

But in '56 Dad moved us east
from that sublime,
through Texas, to Baltimore,
my marbles treasure somehow left behind.

Sometimes now, I rock and count,
bothering this old memory,
and longing still, as I recall
shots aimed and struck perfectly.

Stopping by Uncle Glyn's Farm

In the summer of '56 we moved again,
this time west to east. I was eleven then.
The two-lane roads got straighter and hotter
the closer we got to Texas. Winston
the schnauzer hugged the door with his paws
and sliced the air with his nose. A state road
led through Abilene and Robert Lee
onto a rougher surface that held
to the quarter-section lines of 1785.
Stray stones and dirt ground to fluff sailed a wake
behind our Plymouth hugging the half-moon
country roads, clawing and jouncing its way.
Till a small oasis—a squat farmhouse,
a patch of grass, noisy chickens scratching
at the yard. A Texas Ash filtered the sun.

The coop's screen door creaked open and the spring
banged back wood on wood. A storm of squawks
and feathers burst out in the henhouse
as I gathered brown eggs from shadowed nests
in the must of hay and dust. At the pond,
Uncle Glyn handed me his .22.
One quick twitch, I bagged the water snake.
I skinned him with my jackknife—maybe a belt?
I climbed the split rail fence and leapt
into the corral, my sneakers sinking
into dirt more used to boots and hooves.
A ram thundered at me. My uncle hollered,
grabbed my collar and yanked me up and away.
I climbed the leaning red tractor rusting
in the grass.
                    All else was fresh—
the garden carrots eased from their beds,

Aunt Billie Doris's breakfast eggs, the air
making a gift of manure and soil
and the presence of animal sounds and scent.

Within the warmth and bleats of grinding,
bearded bodies, I wrestled sheep, unsheared
from sheared, through hours of summer heat.
As a reward, Uncle Glyn hoisted me
onto a stamping horse riled by its bridle.
A whack across the croup startled it
into a frenzied gallop hard and hard
to nowhere. I held the saddle horn so tight
and one foot losing its stirrup and my knees
squeezing hard the rounded ribs and the wind
beating hard and the farrago of hooves
and wind, and losing my high-crowned hat
pounding the trail, Hopalong Cassidy
high up on Topper.

We left one morning, on through Oklahoma,
Arkansas, Tennessee, on to the east coast,
reversing one family's centuries-old stream
to the west. We would never return,
but every day, I wear mother-of-pearl
snap shirts with Barstow pockets like Uncle Glyn's
and a hat like his too that can shade
the eastern sunrise as well as sunset
beyond the Rockies.
                              I might have lived tall
like a saguaro, its roots spreading close
to the surface, close to hooves and rain.
I might have lived weathered and quiet
with a horse named Thunder who would trot me home
to a covered front porch, a lucky horseshoe
hung high over the door.

Double Digit Birthday

This day's early morning, sixty years ago,
the boy woke to the thrill of double digits.

He threw on his Levis, pockets jammed
with marbles, keepsies and hard-won aggies.

The day's rising sun nibbled the nubby chairs,
tuft by tuft. In the window, a bud-laden bough.

He hoped for another silver dollar or
a Topps Ted Williams card with bubble gum.

This day this later morning, the light grays
through window smudge, inscribes the silken strand

a spider's spun, the way new-fallen snow
frosts wires reticulating darkened skies.

My hand idles a pocket, jogs loose
the joy of marble-finger shuffling home

from playground sport. Grown children smile
parental from the walls. They'll call today.

I startle in the mirror at a slant-browed hint
of boy. I raise a mottled hand

—it was the boy's—and remember his hopes.
A Babe Ruth bat, a Fijian stamp, mint.

Bank Shot

I asked about the old days, when they
were my age—my mother scrambling eggs,
Dad and I at the table. He aimed a glance
sidelong at her, then took a shot toward me:

We've been very lucky, Son.

He must have meant their gamboling, teenage
marriage after weeks of jitterbug jokes
and getting-to-know-you's in the Abilene
Lady Luck pool hall in 1941.

Her silence like the hush of a tournament
match, the cue's tip skittish at the ball,
probing for angle and spin, velocity,
the all-important leave and follow-on.

By now—both gone so long, both unlucky—
I understand his game, how words can
travel in disguise, their spin covert,
as on that morning when his mumbled plea

caromed off me—sharply, as off
a felted cushion—and spun toward her,
determined at the stove:

Come on, Honey, let's play.
Let's keep the run alive.

Treasure

My mother sent me out for milk, two blocks
right, she said, one left, first time by myself.
I skipped and jumped, avoiding cracks,
fiddled pocketed marbles all the way.
At the market, a gray man on the bench,
dog tags dangling from a leathered neck.
Unshaved and gaunt in a drooping brown suit,
he offered cupped hands to me,
a heap of silver eagles, nickel buffalo,
silver lady dollars sparkling in the sun.
He stared at me, wet mouth
wheezy and open, one gold tooth
which glinted like coins as he thrust his hands
up and up, to me. I stepped away,
near an edge, the man too eager, oddly
friendly, man of no words. I mumbled,
No thank you, exhaled regret. Halfway home,
the glass milk bottle grown heavy, I
sat and leaned back against a tree and thought
about the gray man—whether he had a son
with gold teeth, and why he wouldn't give
his treasure to that son, and why he wasn't
off to work that morning, like my father
whose pocket-change jangled up the walk
home late afternoons, his jaunty stride
and shiny shoes, coins left on the bureau
I could find and rifle through.

Auntie June

For 90 years you never drove, but laughed
your stories of Uncle Lee, how he squired you
through Alaska in a Ford in '41,
to San Diego for my birth in '45.
Stories that spanned the centuries—our westward
family sailing prairie schooners over
dust and swells and scrub, the endless current
rolling on toward Oregon. Your Yorkshire
mother Eliza riding too, each huddling
with the other, as I, a boy, with you.
I polish the length of this old Caddy,
and you emerge, lustrous as midnight
headlights carving deep into the dark.
This last trip looms, a carwash blues,
and still you flaunt and stomp the Charleston
on a Culver City sidewalk, your hair
alive, as in a highway breeze,
aflame in California sun, your full skirt
tossing skeins of Bougainvillea, dropping
petals gracing your long way away.

The Dance

Touching was for marriage, I had learned
at home, and church, so when they gave us lessons
in the gym, I hoped that it would be ok.
Beautiful Simone chose me as her partner,
her skin glowing the soothing olive
of the Sephardim, while I was confused
by the mysteries of attraction: her shapely legs
in algebra, her black hair swept across
her flawless face, a few strands wisping
over one dark eye. The needle dropped,
and the music scratched its way out
of game-score loudspeakers swinging
from the rafters overhead. She stepped
into my arms like a starlet, head tossed,
gazing toward some distant horizon,
our touching of little interest to her,
it seemed. But she pulled me into her warmth,
tight, and oh, the pain—her breast felt
like the sharp nose of a rocket launched
into my chest. It was her gift to me,
while I, in stifled anguish, clenched my teeth
and tried to imagine her fresh young breast,
so close to me then, how nice it might feel
without steel. Only later would I learn
about the fifties' Bullet Bra. One day,
we stepped into an elevator. The doors closed.
We were alone. Her skirt gauzy. Her talk
of training in dance, the strength of her legs.
She said that this, patting one rear cheek,
is the real source of power. I could give it
a feel, she said. Go ahead, she said,
and I did, and I knew, instantly,
that she was right.

Buddies for Life

Squealing rubber slick out of McDonald's,
our gang of four sixteens, two cars, tears north-
east on 413 toward Langhorne, PA,
two yellow lines from south to Bristol Bridge.
I'm propped on a pillow in full command
of my father's red Fury, fins flaming
the Saturday night. Behind, big buddy
Eddie sprawls across the suicide seat
of a Galaxie, Bob manning the wheel.
We're Pro-Keds and gasoline, wind-billowed
collars, single-file on a two-lane road
to Philly pizza, pool hall, girls, who knows?
We do the do-si-do, the pass-lane-pass,
we swim the road's smooth ebb and flow, we whoop
and holler. "Let's Twist Again" clamors from
AM radio. Under stars that flare
through the night sky, our ketchup-stained jeans
jounce Chubby Checker's beat. Crewcuts cruising,
tailpipes blurting, the Galaxie's abreast
my Fury, noses ahead, and again,
again, Bob almost evades the ravine.

Whistled Alive

Late fall, the world again closing in
upon itself. Nights extend, days stall,
and the chill takes hold of Pennsylvania.
We hibernate under artificial light
in the practice room where wrestling coaches
bark enduring truths then whistle us alive
in this rite reserved for the quick, the strong,
the sinewy light doggedly wary.
This must be some kind of love, this shutting out,
shutting in, this drain of self into self,
more weight to shoulder through our hunger.
We shuffle and tender sugarfeet.
He's a mirror-me: I claw, he claws, heads butt,
hands seize sweat-slick muscle. I collar him,
rough a forearm hard to his clavicle,
stutter-step. Balance, balance is all.
I am stronger, faster. So say tight grips,
the hurried brawl. I flash to a leg;
he drops to splay his weight over me,
the way soggy nautical rope might feel —
knotty, tentacular, doughy. He grabs
my head, wheels on the axis he makes of me.
His strength meets mine. I parry his every move
(each the other reified). The mild sorrow
of blood rises warm in my mouth.
He's on his back! I power down, but he rears
unstoppably from the mat. Sudden loss,
sudden win. We practice both, again, again.
No winner here, it's him, myself, I pin.

Blind Date

You rode my bike's crossbar. Campus
was crisp that last college fall. Your hair,
gold and fruity, teased my lips —.

Your scent was close, and far.
Your cardigan lapped at the rise
of my knee. Your plaid skirt swelled in our breeze.

I was pedaling into our future
where you would overcome my awe.
It was a long ride to your room that Saturday night.

I felt your glee all the way.
At the door you drifted to me, close.
We kissed for the first and last time.

Hunted

I eye the stockade fence out back, in season
deep left field, where countless robins perch,
strung out but close, their folded backs to me.
I poke my Daisy BB repeater
out the kitchen window, squint down
the barrel-sight to fix the target,
feathered grey against the blue. A birthright,
it seems to me in the sunshine, to bear arms
in the backyards and alleys of Oregon.

I aim and squeeze and squeeze again, again,
a harmless again, into a hissing wind.
It's play, the fun of the aim and the squeeze,
like Roy Rogers, whose dead guys got back up
and dusted off their chaps. Then a robin
falls. It flutters to the lawn, skitters
in circles and cries, its dangled wing
an open fan, eyes black and blank, red breast
quick-pulsing. And my pink ribby chest

is pulsing. A blanket, a shawl! To somehow
enfold it, to hold it in a safer place to heal
at my hand, eye dropper kerplopping
a meal, from my hand, the drip, the drip
of an IV above the wounded VC,
eyes emptied and lolling, an M-16
fired from under the high, hot azure sky
looming over the paddy, the alley,
their screams, their high, piercing screams.

Precision

The CO screams, "Ten-hut!" We stiffen to stand in rank formation, chins tucked in against Adam's apples. The CO begins to accost us, one by one, flaunting his neatness. Slight, he's a teacup poodle wearing dress blues yapping up at stolid Danes. His shouts at Joe bristle with a certainty I've never known. Joe's name tag's not level with his pocket seam, his hat brim's not shading his nose. My M-1's butt rests in the steady cup of my hand, its barrel stock stiff against my shoulder. It's a preseason game of precision we're likely to lose.

There's a war on in Vietnam that feels somehow wrong. I think of Quemoy, Matsu, Dongding, of folding tables loaded with SDS pamphlets and tended by bearded post-adolescents who shout of injustice and death. At night in the dorm, we talk about death, death as idea, death as encumbrance, death as TV. We want to start, not end, our lives. We bet on ROTC, others on bone spurs or the Navy or Canada or med school. Now I'm Howdy Doody in a shooting arcade who, if shot, will collapse into death, far from the factory that made me.

Uh oh, here's the CO. "Present arms" the poodle shouts at my face. He showers my face, he takes my rifle. "Soldier," he showers again, "what's the serial number of your weapon?" "Sir," I shout, "the serial number of my weapon is 8732234928, Sir!" He glances near the rear sight for confirmation, hands the rifle back, and moves on. He's hassling the next guy about his buttons and haircut when it occurs to me I've just shouted at him my social security number. I don't know why, but I'd like to win this preseason game called *precision* we're likely to lose.

The Home Front

He pumped his fist toward the arcing sky
of National Airport, another diminutive
desk-bound Patton exhorting another
soldier-son to war, playing a role,
a screen-bound Cagney, reality
smoldering at home. My mother pleated her lips.
Her hand trembled a wave slowed by denial,
then sunk by the weight of despair.

Once aboard, I thought of them at home —
he to bed early with Churchill and Twain.
She in the den with *Saturday Review,*
drinking the hours, anesthetized into
the next afternoon. Then the long worry
over the Pacific — avoiding
the fitful eyes of others — as the passage
from family to war passed in a dazzle,
the way a mortar shell streaks through the long
lull between barrel-burst and the shuddered
rending of somebody's home.

In-Country: Day One

Duffel bag stuffed in the back, I bounced down
Cong Ly on the suicide seat. The sergeant crowed
they'd stolen the mud-scarred jeep the night
before on a Cholon whorehouse street.

My starched jungle fatigues and boots were a joke
in a city of thousands, .45 hard
on my hip. Dressed in yellow, Saigon hummed
like a factory. Fuel-stench hung like a scrim.

The sun seared down on angels in *ao dais*,
silk panels in a red soft as wet blood,
in the green of my mother's eyes.
They skimmed the simmering sidewalks,

at ease in their beauty under the palm-leaf
shade of conical *nón lá*, the calm rise
of dry heat, skirts wafting in spiraled mists
of *nuoc mam*, the smog of fried steam rolls.

That night, I sauntered down Tu Do Street.
The bar girls called and the cyclos spat
their two-cycled rasp. Distant iron bombs
dropped from B-52s burst out of the dark,

laying a blanket of moans over me
and the street and the girls too young in the night.
I glanced at the stars and felt myself
holding onto my gun with both hands.

Medevac Chopper

Looking up, it occurs to me,
                    It could be
a hummingbird. The way it floats and quivers
over the clearing.
                    But the rotor blades blow
a storm of wind that howls the dust and pebbles,
pelts our eyes, ripples the paddy beyond.
Settling from side to side, surfing a shaft
of driven air, its blast spasms and flattens
high grass until the skids jolt onto the pad.

Now we rush as a scrum into the clamor,
bend to the force pushing at our chests,
reach into the cargo bay and find the war
delivered again to our hands, soldiers
on stretchers arrayed like logs. One leads,
one follows, hefting the load, schlepping
to the ER, which is tethered to weather
the gale, its air-stiffened walls trembling ahead.

Our sweaty hands slip round the wood handles,
the whipped air now at our backs. Wounds weep
and pool on bellies, and with each strike
of each boot, IV lines swing wild in the wind.
Off duty later, we peel away
our fatigues and closely inspect
an arm, a leg, our own shaven heads.

The Operating Room

A chopper pounds the baking air,
muffled fading, as the mess hall's
evening siren sounds. Surgical
nurses scuttle down the wooden
sidewalk, which bridges mud and puddles
to the O.R., where I lock
my heavy tripod legs in place,
insert a fresh magazine,
zoom in:
        Like a half-eaten
pomegranate left for sniffing dogs,
the boy lies open in Da Nang,
five surgical teams scratching
at his flesh, harsh lights tracing
paths the shrapnel took when his boot
landed on the mine. Blood spatters
the lens, gushes over gloved hands
incising, sawing, full-stroked through
fresh-grown limbs, the labored heaving
laid raw beneath what's left
of pink skin, a one-limb body
without privates or a face.
Safe behind my camera,
I murmur at the crimson
saturation, the perfection
of the angle. I lean high
over the surgeon's shoulder—
nearly breach the sterile field
sliding the 16-millimeter
Arriflex from the thoracic
to the maxillo-facial
grazing the meticulous debride.
The limb-site surgeons grow testy.

At last, a slowing slap of stainless
instruments against open palms
signals the waning night, fewer
fluids to be hung and replaced.
Still, there beats a heart they won't let quit.
Final suture sewn, instruments
and camera stowed, the boy wheeled away,
the slumping, the heavy, bloodshot,
we drag on to breakfast, gritting
our teeth against the unsaid hope
he'll die.

Army Photographer, Research Dermatologist

Rice fields washed and bent in the choppered
ruckus, the Delta fleeting beneath our boots,
we slowed into the settling of our own din,
onto the clearing, the sand-bagged base camp
like a Hollywood set, the scene morose
with soldiers who littered scrubby flatland.
We were REMFs, rear-echelon
motherfuckers, come to survey how they
might survive. Doc asked one soldier how many
days he'd slogged through paddies, slept wet
in fatigues and socks, how many leeches
he'd burned from his crotch. Doc turned to the sole
and heel and toes of a kaleidoscopic foot,
its welter of colors. *Wow! Get a close shot
of this!* Eye rapt in my viewfinder,
I marveled at fungal shadows,
scattered islands across the arch, the ankle,
under nails, the foot bloated, blue currents
coursing beneath yellow-purple knolls.
Wow, I thought, *Wow!* then snapped.

Huey Chopper

Beneath its
metronomic
pounding
its eddied scorch
of driven air,
black boots
dangle over Nam,
low enough
to clip
rice plants near
harvest height
ahead, their swollen
grain at sway
in summer's
dance until,
Huey-startled, they
fall,
slammed flat, the
paddy,
so riven
it seemed then
it could never mend.

Urgencies

I choppered in and out among
the grunts, the coarsened kids
slouched in grease and M-16s,
who might instead have prowled
the paved two lanes called 413,
Langhorne to Bristol PA,
in throaty Bonnevilles.
I preferred my episodic terror
to their numbing hum and drum,
every moment gravid with alarm,
but embraced their comforts—
dry clothes and shaded ground, latrines
dug recently, and mostly, for me,
the sylph who shed her palm-leaf
nón lá and fluttered to me fresh
from paddy muck, her silk *ao dai*
twinkling through dim paper light,
who might instead have met
a boy from the nearby village,
a boy she might have embraced
one sun-seared day like all the rest
in a patch of maiden grass
just off the path uniting them.

Chow Time

From out of the perfect dark,
incoming just past midnight,
whistling mortars weave-walk
through camp, dropping luck
and boom onto this hooch
or that. In the morning mess
we're sullen, shuffling for food
spooned out of mermite cans.
Most silent, some mumblers
hardly heard, hardly there.
One harbors jarred-ear souvenirs.
Another, spent cartridges.
We live the real unreal
every day, X each out at night.
Once down to double digits,
we think our luck may hold
after all — if paddy stench
and heat, dense and mean,
don't roast us first. We nurse
word wounds that piss us off
and hard-hammered wounds
from shrapnel and dings on the job.
And all is shades of dirt
in this foreign scrub of land,
and our faces grey, our shoulders
stooped in olive fray. We clutch tin pots
hot with rations. One guy mutters
in a semi-southern slur,
"Ain't no shit like this back in the world."

Super Bowl III

"I'm short," we say, counting down the days
one by one deep into our full year's tour,
till we will return, as we like to say,
"back in the world," to Newark or Galveston.

Where no CO or lifer will decide
what our chances might be this day or next.

Where no small-boned, lean-muscled men
labor on docks through the heat of the day
and might loft grenades from the cool of the night.

Where no bar girls gesture with delicate wrists
to offer themselves as "Number 1! Cheap!"

Where no APO letters arrive
to say "Your grandfather died."

Where no buddies carry hacked-off
VC ears preserved in squat jars.

Where Radio Saigon delivers the news
from Woodstock, Country Joe and the Fish,
their "What're we fightin' for," the first
moon landing, the Jets beat the Colts.

"Back in the World"

What we slurred in passing, quieting
unvoiced longing, till it garnished, then ladened

the everyday—tasteless, hardly there
in a where that seemed hardly real, blurred

as if we'd been cast as bit players
in a movie for which suspension

of disbelief came hard, a movie glaring
and roaring of choppers and bombers

and bombs and the whistle of shards, making
a soundtrack of the absurd in the heat

and paddy stench, jungle stench, the stench-cloud
of cyclos, a persistent other that, a lifetime

later, still shades and crowds their world, its lore,
this world, which no longer resembles

the world we longed for when young and other.

Binh

The boy's mother held him,
held his lolling head. Strands
of her straight black hair
lay matted in gullies of tears.
Her wails surfed the quavering walls
of the 27th MASH unit
in Chu Lai. He must have been
nearly two, barely conscious.
A pretty, bronze child. All day,
the surgeon had opened
GI chests, debrided those
and other wounds, sawed then closed
arms and legs, rushed from bed
to bed. Stumps and slings and
gauze-wrapped skulls—now this boy.
He felt sure he could re-plumb,
make him whole for whatever
this place might become.
The surgery went well, and the boy
did well for hours in post-op.
Binh died in the early morning,
and the surgeon cried, and
another medevac chopper arrived.

The Upshot

For all the post-coital years that remained,
there were nightmares, as if the heaven

of love's aftermath had been denied him
whose crime lay in surviving the firefights,

his buddies de-legged, de-armed, de-lifed.
There's a calculus of sleep at work —

the reward for killing and dying,
a long, obliterative sleep;

for killing and living, the knife-edged sleep
of alarm, an omigod kind of sleep;

for not killing and living — unfired rifles
quiet beside sheeted bunks, bar girls nearby —

no nightmares, no swim through night sweats.
Untroubled, but for the occasional flinch,

and the dead weight of that dreadful word, veteran.

Service

Santa had one dented cheek.
Then church. And after the singing along
from the red brick of a book,

there was up-and-downing, praying,
flying angels, trumpets long silent, manger,
thunderous organ, Jesus in sandals.

My mother's white-gloved hand held my hand
and led me down the crowded aisle toward the door
where the pastor, bent slightly, offered his hand,

cassock hanging to the floor like a lady's gown.
Laying his hand on my neatened head, his voice
slid over me like silk over a girl's shoulder,

"I can see that this is a very good
little boy." I thought so, but how could he know?
I could be dressed for the part, but planning

to kick another bad boy when I got home.
I think of that pastor now when someone says,
"Thank you for your service."

Hearth War

A long gray whine sears through the intermittent
sizzle of these winter flames writhing by my chair.

Memory's mortar whistles alarm immortal
as this war tome saddles my lap and strains

and seethes to tell me what I know but can't
follow—my compass another casualty.

Its pages, spitting embers of war, insist
on what's elusive, the heart of the matter,

their voice a target, as other voices
brawl from another room, jets thunder above,

radios buzz, trucks grumble by outside,
and from below, the dryer tumbles, tumbles.

Earline

She looks out from the forties' photograph
in the ostentatious health of a southern girl
with the toothsome smile of Miss America,
filling her blouse, a hand-me-down from sister
Billie Doris, maybe Maxine. Her brunette *do*
gleams, a full skirt cinches her waist,
and a careful hand, slight at her face, frames
one lazied-down eye, a sweetheart wink
in the heat and dust far out on the edge
of a used-up Texas town. During the war,
even the poorest sort of girl in the plainest
sort of dress, who posed leaning back
against the only tree for miles, could blaze
in dry heat like a breeze-rocked apple.
The buses carried bib-overalled boys
to Camp Bowie, Camp Swift. On three-day pass,
sporting white sidewalls, garrison caps
raked to one side, they would come and go, base
to home, then to Europe or the Pacific,
an army that moved in time to Artie Shaw's
jukebox clarinet. A sergeant from Idaho
caught her eye in Abilene. Short but strong,
he sang his own song, they began to beguine,
she left technical school, thirty years slipped by,
God left town for good, her brother died,
kids weren't the same, even her own, and the world
got big, until, bewildered, she steered
the '68 Plymouth in woozy aim
straight at the hardened heart of that lying tree.

The Silence

Ever been clobbered
by a wraith?
Me neither. Till
a drawn-back sheet
revealed her face,
unlined and wreathed
in hair still black,
scattered over
stainless steel.
She, mute as ever
in the half a life
she had, summoned
the power she never had
and hacked off my legs.
I scuffed into dawn,
lost in the tombstones,
feeling my way toward
what's moot but persists.
In a grove of ashes,
the little left of me
lay in the weeds and soot,
till the lilies wilted
in the chill and died,
and I, too late to hear
what she left unsaid.

Porcelain

I

Silent and fine as the blood-red vase
perched on our living room mantel, you waved,

your white-gloved hand laboring goodbye
in surrender. By your side, Dad, in uniform,

gleamed in ramrod triumph. I drifted vaguely
into a fog, down the ramp, to my flight,

brooding my way: How would you survive
the coming year, when broken bodies would litter

my letters home and *Life* would luster its pages
with two hundred forty-two faces in "One Week's Toll"?

II

Rigid, upright, your posture had always seemed
more pose than poise. Dad tiptoed around you,

his ceramic doll. Your glaze dulled my years.
You careened through opaque perils,

always tense, brittle, tilting at the edge,
when I felt a closing in, the air

sucking thin. Boy-busy, what did I know
of hidden bottles? Then, home from college

one night: you, my lissome mother,
tottering like a vase in jeopardy,

primly louche in the frame of my door.

Greg with father, Mickey, and mother, Earline

Greg, mother, and sister, Rhondda, about to leave for Yokohama

Greg with his father, circa 1984

Greg and Rhondda, their father, and their children, Lang and Danny

Bright Bird

Beneath the hot sting, the seamless drone, I'm shrouded by clouds, wet walls, no sound but this, an other world entire, and you reify from its mist as one of the countless streams that steam onto my bending back, and my heart takes one of those deep dives—a son is shot, a mother dies—yet, I linger at the precipice of your dimples, implausibly deep, filled with expectation of laughs and love and luck to come after your harrowing flight through sixteen years, which stopped, just stopped, bright bird, stout wall, and I'm fumbling for soap that wants to dive, and I turn to face the void, where you remind me what a perfect place the shower is to cry.

But Will

I have only red roses this Mother's Day
for her who once was my world, who still

cleaves close as the fragrant fog that shrouds
these weathered stones, she who gave

a lonely love in her short time.
I do not want to join her, but will,

first in felt absence, soon unremembered
as the single petal fallen into tall grass

on that memorable day in May
I last gave into her tender arms

Obsession Red Roses, ribboned and bowed
in their delicacy, their treachery,

and some bulbs, imminent with profusion,
a long-stemmed bouquet, as I recall.

Lookin' Good

I am saying your words, I am
saying your words—Damn!—I am
wheezing, your hand heavy at my chest,
your golden-boy hair sloughing off suns
that warm and stun me to the wall,
crying Damn! saying your song.

I am walking your walk, I am
walking your walk, saunter and strut,
'cause you're proud and young and in some luck,
Texas starlet on your arm (mother to come),
and I know your knowing—you own
that knowing—Damn, you're lookin' good!
A little short, biceps and pecs, the Kid
at ease, Lucky Strikes and aviator shades.
Damn! Who knows what you might have been
with more luck?

I am thinking your thoughts, I am
thinking your thoughts, like De Niro
living his lines, and checking my pocket
where I kept her love safe for me, kept
her safe from the filth of this world,
from memories of dust and broken horses.
But destroy herself? Goddamn!
I did not know (you could not know)
and on the slick of time I held
my ground, but just, and Son?—Damn!
Damn!—Who knew? Who knew how?

The Visit

Dad: silver-haired, widower,
post-stroke. "Hello, Son."

The embrace: foreign,
yet familiar,

one of those things
you don't forget, but don't

remember knowing.
His breadth amazed me

once again, my greeting arms
unequal to the task.

Fated to fit within his grasp,
I felt him swallow my small frame.

At 35, still and forever
the boy, my head landed

on his massive shoulder.
Still and forever strong,

he gave a squeeze that spoke
regret. And now he's gone.

All Went Well

A drainage hose snakes from the hole
in his neck. A nurse steers his gurney.
Wincing, he waves, flashes a grin.
Everybody's friend, always ready for a game,
he loves puns and kids, he's liberal with clichés.
Even on his back, he's combustible.
He slides into the maw of 50-50.
I am unfazed: I have mastered
my father's lessons in denial.

The hours drip, drip.

Then the doctor's in the corridor,
green scrub cap, surgical mask tendriled
onto his chest.

All went well . . .
we began to suture, but
couldn't stop the bleeding,
and we lost him.

And the floor gives way. Light dust mattes its sheen.
The doctor wears brown shoes. A broom bristles
toward me. A custodian, smooth dancer
on linoleum, keeps time pushing the push broom,
we lost him, we lost him, we lost him . . . .

A Body Lay

A body lay in a casket
dressed in my father's dress blues,
sporting double braided cord in gold,

the mouth placid as satisfaction.
Multi-colored rows above one pocket
defined a well-ribboned life.

The silver hair matched shiny eagles,
stern at each shoulder, which ordered
the brass-button soldiers to hold

and attend the body whole.
There were flags, horses, a caisson,
testimonials, gunfire and Taps.

I kissed the hard cold forehead.
How might it have gone
if sometimes he'd worn other clothes?

Sizes

My sister found our father's ring,
turquoise faded, sullied silver-plate.

It stopped my breath. Thirty years ago
I took it from his cold hand.

A big man, he never took it off,
not when he dug or swung or swam,

or smeared on huckleberry jam,
or held a cribbage peg, or gripped

a favorite pitching wedge, then fudged
his score again. With feeling,

she placed it on my palm,
we his keepers. I slipped it on.

It hung, slack, wanting more.
It stung. Once, the shoes. Now this.

I'm Old, I Hear Things

Deck chimes chime and sing
of early rain. The TV drones
of rockets, of new old stars
still silent, still to be named.
My voiceless mother sounds
my name while I arrange
what's left of the hollow
that was home. Their frayed chair
winces as I sit, their table moans.
Strung laser-like from one old war
to now, the live-wire fire
of tinnitus stridulates
in fixed-track monotone.
China clatters to the table,
a ruckus he would hate;
in our house there could be
but one ruckus-maker
of the plates. Knives scrape
across her raised gold leaf.
Louder still, her absence.

Collisions in Slow Motion

An SUV turned into the wrong lane,
and time slowed into the steamy day.

Its impassive headlights came at me
sitting on my scooter at the stop sign.

It came with a screech of speed slow time
had tamed to frame by frame. I watched it come,

I might live or die. The impact razed
my idling reverie. Like that early marriage

lives ago, I watched its dissolution
coming at me, slowed as red lava flows,

I powerless to make it stop. And my mother,
slow year after year of misery and drink,

kept coming in her long, slow slide to suicide,
her hollowed eyes like burnt-out headlights.

Dear Mom

You span a near century, the forty-nine years
you lived, the forty-nine I've given you life.

That first year, I bargained for more,
and now I have hope — quantum theory

says that things can exist simultaneously
in two places, maybe more.

UFOs may be real, and space-time thinking
accommodates the idea of time travel.

Since the impossible now seems possible,
I'm writing to you. Delivery may be difficult —

I'm hoping the impossible will help me out.
Life was so hard for you. I'm glad you lived

to see me safely home from war, where your war
to be a woman who counted was so hard

in those days. At least you finally found some peace.
Thank you for loving me. I miss you, Mom.

Now thirty years older than those you lived,
I'm open to any possibility.

If there's a way, please give me a call
or drop me a line. An email or text would do.

Freight

When a boy, and young man, I rode the trains
along both coasts and the inland trains
through steel towns and coal towns and still feel
the lulling clack of jointed rail pulsing
through plush seats and berths, through me,
and with me on into the night heading home
from school, or to see a girl, or go to war,

or I hoist myself into the shadows
of a boxcar standing alone at the edge
of town, sheltering freight stacked high —
our home too cold, too hot, neckties
absurdly thin, my whittling father
whistling at time and stumbling deeper
into deepened dark, the timbre
of my kid-sister's sounds filtering down
from her upstairs nest and the kiltered gait
of a war-dead friend, though each visit veils
more and further until steel wheels ache
into motion, the locomotive heaves,
towing the boxcar, jostling side to side
through the switch onto the main line, the train
accelerating into time, mileposts blurring
the past behind, streaking over the smooth-
railed roadbed, chasing west toward forgotten.

Marriage 70s Style

"What kind of man's no bigger than his wife?"
She lights scented candles, wears beaded belts

and hand-sewn sandals. She's incensed. He's unhip,
bewildered. (She wants to slip him in her purse,

a small piece of home for when she steals out
at night in that scarlet sheath he likes.)

She's unraveling who she's been and what it was
they were, and now, she's shaving round her pubes

for the first time. He brushes his teeth,
pays the bills, feeds the dogs. All he is or

isn't, does or doesn't, rouses her distaste,
dims the memory of his touch, his puns,

his parking luck, incites that special hate
we save for those we know too well.

Moving Day

It was a moving day, the barn-raising
commune of that time. Afterward, we all

milled about her new apartment, mugs and
stemware in hand, and talked of jobs and songs,

Sgt. Pepper's Band. We were grad students,
some post-war, most pre-children. Her stuff

was boards, bricks, a platform bed, books and beanbags.
A smoking, single mother in motion and crisis.

Her little girl—coiled on hands and knees,
a sky-blue-eyed three-year-old, her hair

feral tangles of silvered-gold—mugged up
at me, tugging hard at some part of me

I didn't know I had. That part yielded
all of me, which dove to hands and knees,

where we scuttled and growled over the carpet,
she and I, among chair legs, argyles, penny loafers,

the languorous legs of comely young mothers.
Overhead, they smoked sang-froid, they sipped

of cool, they slid on early disco. It was all
easy give and take. I could've stood, but didn't.

Second Tie

We coaxed a clerk into
June sun on the Ellicott City
courthouse lawn where she summoned
the law out of air alive in light
just right for making new
lives gone awry, you and I,
man and wife, newly tied
till death do us part,
you, working woman
in pale salmon-red dress,
clutching baby's breath,
your small children huddled
close, and I, wildly hirsute,
a bit fuddled perhaps,
wide-tied and cool in canary
yellow linen, wide-toed shoes,
psychedelic purple peonies
spilling willy-nilly from
the acreage of my new tie.

Pram

Newborn baby boy aboard, I steered
our second-hand umbrella stroller
onto Woodside. I didn't see
the layered, floating clouds,
didn't hear the non-swivel wheels
squealing, the plastic hubs rattling.

My hands quiver with the murmur
of a royal Silver Cross Balmoral,
which I guide by its swan-neck handle,
its fat-tube, cream-colored tires rolling
under a sky so clean its blue-white
shines.
        O, to stroll
my infant son in a coach-built pram
crowned by its quarter-moon bonnet,
its hand-sprung, strap-hung chassis
bobbing above chrome wheels, spokes arcing
late sun, gliding the hours, then dimming,
rolling desultorily between
tall brick homes receding into
the dusk as the streetside gas lamps
rouse themselves, one by one,
a procession of small suns glimmering
into twilight. Then horses' hooves
clopping over the cobblestones
pulling dainty carriages home
from The City.
        O, to nod
left and right in time to a song
I hum, like Bing Crosby crooning
a tossed-off tune from a warm
tube radio, the willows sweeping
low before this son, this son
of all sons, this prince receiving his due.

Side by Side
at the Zoo

We're standing together,
but he looms above me,

and I crane to get
a better look at him,

the same brown eyes,
a now-bony face etched

against the high blue sky.
He's an Adam's-appled hawk

who needs a shave, I notice,
my lanky, angular son,

his arm slung avuncular
over my shoulder,

mere moments since he
straddled the saddletree

crook of my narrow hip
—I, his rearing pony—

when he clung to me snug
as a tree-snoozing chimpanzee,

content to ride me anywhere.

More

Another day devolves to ritual:
Playful, I ring the doorbell of our home,

fumble glove-handed for the key, enter,
my heart, from deep, mid-winter dark. Before

I lay aside my hat and heavy coat,
I find you at the stove. I love the tilt

of your lips to mine, your green-eyed lanterns
that signal yes. Our kiss lingers, a link

purled forward from nights thirty years ago.
Your gas-flamed pans crackle and spit high heat.

Your sautéd Porcini mushrooms compete
with my desire, the night spread before us,

soup exquisite with Vidalia onion,
prelude to the interplay of voices

voicing more than all we've said before,
the way our kisses lead to more, the way

your soup's the same but always better,
like our nights. There's always more.

Spooning

A spoon
lies sturdy
in repose,
its arc of
neck like
yours, and
yields to
my light
touch—
a finger
slide
along
the
nape
down
down
to
ample
bowl.
See how
yours and mine,
on edge, married tip
to heel, lie as if designed
to meet in this satin box
in such economy of
space, and so met,
to sleep.

Before Night Falls

Before night falls, and soon,
a damask sky but blue

lights intermit dimmed air
like stars, and blue consumes

the yielding day as seas
receive new fallen rain

as soil receives a seed

within its folds and holds
all possibilities, and

as blue resolves this day
I dream the coming hours

the way we'll ride this sky
once more, soft hands, you and I.

Strangers

Morning. We stand on the front porch, looking out
over the familiar brick and green, and farther on,
to the sun-frosted horizon. Our English boxwood
line and scent the path below, so broad
in their old age that we must sidle our own
widened selves against the stiff-leaved narrow.
The familiar has grown strange, the way our children
grew in stealth, day by day, into their own
becoming. I remember our first night—
Luigi's swarthy waiters bearing
steaming bowls of pasta and puttanesca,
and you, a stranger to me among friends,
bent in the remnants of beautiful sorrow,
alone, like me, alone in the time of desire.
We are not as we were, and I wonder,
can our amended selves learn to live,
to live well, one with the other, now,
when learning comes less easily. I summon
something like faith that this path will lead
to possibility. I take your hand
in mine. Come, I want to find you again.
Kiss me, I whisper through my greed.

Shoulders

Tasseled curtains rustle
daybreak air which gentles us

inaudibly this stone-cool morning.
Languid as a swelling sea,

I sigh and roll to her.
I kiss a memory, a shoulder

—bare, chaste. The man I was
I am, risen to another day

in which she travels where I go.
I chase her through the waves

of love's long-tossed affairs
and would catch her if I could,

and my young man. They,
slipping through time-stricken air,

reach out to me as they recede.
I covet that somewhere

where the man I was I am
where in our sacred disarray

I kiss a shoulder—bare, less chaste.

Diminished

I stride into the mists and disappear.
—Edwin M. Zimmerman,
1924–2012

It was a good thing
to tell his story
with our stories,
each of us
one thin strand of who
and what he was,
and he for me
a keeper of the best
of who I am.
But keepers fade
away, one, then one,
a piece of me
tucked under an arm,
his story, my story,
that intersection
now closed. I turn onto
Woodside Parkway,
take the detour,
and hope that when
I get home, someone
will know who I am.

Red Brick Houses

See you tonight. Briefcase in hand, I kiss
my wife, this other life, and trace the path
down weather-speckled concrete steps onto
the street where other red brick houses sit,
posted face to face, just as when we moved in.
The years turn and turn till momentum fuels
my walk along this trail flanked by stoic trees,
sentinels poised before the parade that straggles by.
House windows gape, opaque, as I march
block to block through November's morning chill.
All's ice-still. I know this street too well—
the garage ahead that signals where the road-
way edge falls away, where the corner
neighbor's hedge of yews points the way to town.
I think of archaeologists someday fussing
with picks and shovels and brushes. What
will they make of this crumbled asphalt
winding by foundations ancient
as the Black-Eyed Susan seeds left sprinkled
by the side, these clues of us? Who were they,
what did they want, these orderly people?
White clouds string out and hover in the dawn,
an archipelago of islands on a sky
so clean its blue-white seems wet with artist's paint.
Retirement rides my mind like an overladen
truck. I'm tired. From a mile ahead the railroad
drones its clack-clack song and calls me to
its straightaway: *Come, these trains can take you,
once again, to where you've never been,
where sloughing trees and light recede,
and they will bring you back again to where
you'll never leave, back to red brick walls
that may stand just long enough.*

Sidewalk

"Got a little change, Gramps?"
How's he know? Our kids
no longer slide the hill out front,

no longer live at home.
Their babies tug our hearts,
my wife no longer walks,

and love for us remains the same, but
not. So, yeah, my friend,
a little change I've got.

Work

Here's Jim from the city before sunrise,
no hat, no jacket, no tools, half my age,
twice my size. He surveys the waste of weeds
and ivy overrunning my backyard. I'll buy
some Black-eyed Susan seeds. He digs and prunes,
lifts and hauls, crafts mounds of trash all afternoon.
As he rakes my clay-creased soil, each tine
tills a narrow furrow. He plies the wooden
garden hoe like a surgeon and muscles
blackened mulch into a state of repose,
draping the beds my mind's eye sees
so clearly.
       My Grandfather Sören,
a Danish foreman, for fifty years
did what needed doing at the Snake River dam
and power plant. My father laid concrete,
repaired the roof, fixed the stove, built a trellis
and brick wall, all on weekend time, while I
read or dreamed or played some ball. Now, Triple A
changes my flats, fixes whatever else
needs fixing at the time. My own current project
is searching for the hammer and hooks
I lost track of about a year ago
when I meant to hang those family pictures
still on the floor, tipped against the bedroom wall.

An Idea

Under the covers,
our bodies fitted
as if for shipping,
my hand browses
your wrist, and you,
traces our story
to this very night
in this long-loved room
where my idea
of me has changed
along the way,
but my idea
of you
—spun from scraps
of this and that
from what I was
and who I found
forty years ago—
I hold
with all the might
I may still have.
That idea held dear,
I draw you close.

Speed

I'm an old guy in my den, a slow guy
these days, reading, writing, sometimes glancing

at paneled walls laden with my stilled life—
kid pictures, plaques of law, war photographs.

Through the front window, I catch a glimpse
of a young guy crouched on slick, ball-bearing

wheels hurtling down the long, deep-sloping street.
A free-wheeling guy who has found the glee,

the narcotic risk, of speed. My risk
is at home, trudging up and down slick stairs

hauling trash, retrieving the ice-crusted
morning paper. Risk in the gathering

tempo of age. Risk in remembering:
speeding the coast, the Southern Pacific,

in a sleeping berth, when I was a boy,
so like a dream, speeding into the night,

the lull of click and clack and smoky horn.

Needlepoint Swans

When the kids were kids
when the kids were parents

bedtime paramount
bedroom intimate as we

below our framed needle-
point swans, chatting our day

I reading Roth, you McEwan
flicking off our lamps

arranging our bodies
onto our left sides

toward the next day's more
arm sliding round hip and waist

hand cupping your breast
whisper kisses to your neck

grazing the hairline,
finally spooning into dream

in the way, in the beginning,
your girlfriend assured

"he'll get over that."
But I never did.

Sunny

1986–1998

Your burly paws dangle from the porch.
You keep your eye on neighbors passing by
your turf. I step out and rattle the leash.
Your tail sweeps the concrete, and your front paws
push right, left, in a shuffle against your weight.
And you rise. Let's go, old boy. Let's ease on down,
down the front yard path, the parkway slope, leashed
one to the other. You take our moonlit walk
with a labored plod, nails scraping the asphalt,
tail dragged low. You pause to inspect but one
or two trees of the redolent world
only you know and show little joy this night
of wispy clouds and shivers. We turn back
where the lace leaf maple spills its shredded skirt.
But you stumble. You heave. Like a child,
your eyes seek mine. You careen back home
and drop to the lawn as if struck a vicious blow.
I reel inside I pace beside your bowl and bed
the golden strands you've shed I can't seem to find
my way in the house I give a raspy shout
Sunny's not well and now we're moving
I won't remember how from a living room
to a door and you're missing I'm unsteady
I look down for firm level ground and there
spot you below on the porch somehow you're home
slack-jawed facing the street still, still
as a bronzed lion dangling burly paws.

My Pilot

Zach is four. Son of my son, like his father,
he knows what we're to do. In the playroom downstairs,
we read the Berenstain Bears, then it's Chutes
and Ladders. A bear stalks by. A bear?
No matter. He whispers, "Bopa. Pretend."
The door to his playhouse is open. "Oh no,
I'm allergic to crocodiles, and he's gone!"
We scan the landscape. "Oh no, the cow
is gone too! He's on the moon!"
Now we're a train chugging around
the blackboard easel, down the hall,
to the backroom where his astro tent
is pitched, resplendent with stars, planets, rockets.
He scrambles in, flips onto his back
into the pilot seat. I crawl in too,
we face the moon; our mission: bring back the cow.
The thunder of propulsive engines
drives us up and off the pad. Smooth sailing
all the way, we land. I guard the rocket.
Zach bounces across the pocked surface.
In no time, he's got the cow stuffed
into the cargo hold. We high-five,
flip the switch, and zoom back to planet earth.
We herd the cow back into the playhouse.
Zach pulls out his many dinosaurs.
T-Rex, Stegosaurus, Giganotosaurus,
Supersaurus, Triceratops. He matter-
of-factly recites the names and corrects
my pronunciations. "This is better,
Bopa. Since you're over Covid, I can
hug you again." And just in time, as now
it's time for me to go home for my nap
and to dream of falling through a ship's porthole
into the roiling Pacific and, thanks
to passing driftwood, finding my way back home.

Kitchen Cabinets

The kitchen cabinets persist in their rise
toward irrelevance, and shelves below

sink into the inaccessible. Across
this cold winter, my spirit snowshoe-trudges

toward some slow end where even the warmth
has lost its warmth. The streets grow long.

Fewer novels read as novel,
and the daily news redunds ad infinitum.

I hold to what will not repeat itself:
my youngest grandson squirming on my lap

here at home, singing at the kitchen table
while I hold his dripping ice cream cone,

now melting toward its own slow end.

The Widowed Brides
of Woodside

In the blue-grey cool of morning, I amble
down the weathered stepping stones, retrieve
the morning paper. Across the street,
our neighbor, Tom, emerges with his small twins
who quickly set about to fill the day
with evidence of themselves—their thinly high
and loud hellos, their tree-limb swinging,
soccer kicking. Tom cradles his Post
and waves, as I first waved to Petie
thirty years ago, tending that same yard.

She and other widowed brides of Woodside,
— Kitty, Louise, Mrs. Corey and Esther—
wove their way within our lives, watching
our three children, trading books, sharing
seasonings for Chesapeake blue crab.
Some summer evenings, as dusk settled
unhurriedly, Petie would call us over
for Chardonnay and evening primroses
that yawned awake in dwindling yellow haze.

Climbing the steps back to our door, *Post*
in hand, I imagine sixty years ago,
perhaps another blue-grey day like this,
when Petie moved into her new house
where she made a home for her children,
who like her would thrive, and for her husband,
John, who would die too soon.

Walking to Another Life

I took a different route a few blocks over
and came upon a neighbor I didn't know.
She strolled, leash in hand, an unleashed vibrance
in her step, yet an easy style in holding
to the road. I asked about her dog,
a Pembroke Corgi, a well-groomed little guy.

We started to chat, as neighbors do
when chance aligns and there is time.
I felt no tension such as often comes
when male meets female, man admiring,
woman pleased, yet guarded. She made sure
to say how much her fifteen-year-old boy
loves the dog. A small and aged man,
I took as sly flattery that it might occur
to her that I could harbor designs.
She could be my granddaughter.

She and I crossed paths again another
happy day, and our conversation turned
to novels and public policy.
And by then, I was in love. Perhaps
a bit sly myself, I said, "I hope
that if we meet in another life
we'll be closer in age and you'll accept
my invitation to dinner." "How sweet
of you," she said, "but I think there will be
no other life for us. I'm happy in this one,
as I hope for all good men such as yourself."
My inchoate hopes for new life dashed
again, I said, "And how kind of you
to appear to me in this one."

I Haven't Been Able
to Write About It

This coupling we do. The time of it. The angst
of it. The frenzied love of it. The children,

the commute, the move to Oregon
that never happened. My Harris Tweed and hat.

Your soft, salmon-colored dress. The scent
of morning eggs. Your body, my body,

our bed. The road trips, our incessant talk.
Memories blurred by time—a dulling sense of time.

Time now to clip your nails, to change your sheets
and negligee, to wash your hair, and when dry,

to brush the fullness of it, the white whiteness
of it, hair that sparkles in any kind of light,

hair that upended the drama of its glossy
blackness, that raced the swerves and winds

of the Pacific Coast Highway, almost
careless through the silvery light at Big Sur,

your eyes big, their wholesome greenery,
my scoff at enlightenment in Esalen.

Time casts its light forward into
the at-first unfelt dawn of its ebbing,

deep into the modest light of hope
and small pleasures, of the coming

uncoupling of that coupled self we were.

Heart Attack

It begins with the one you hold closest,
the one on whom you have staked your one life,

just the smallest letting go, the way words
lift off a page in the fog of dim light,

till the terrible gentleness gives way,
and it's more like the trembling Dear John

from your first great love when at war,
when 23, when the long days slowed

in leaden sorrow, or worse, like your body-
gone-wobbly-with-age ripped from the self

you've become, with your one, and you are pierced
hot with the ache of unquiet sleep,

and your heart beats the hurt harder, faster,
then softer, slower, till you know

it's near empty of beats, the way even
the greatest love story blurs to its final words.

Women Dancing
on My Grave

I hope it's dignified.
Flowers strewn, loose
at the base.
Late light splintered
through striations
of feathered clouds.
Maybe birdsong,
contrapuntal,
yet a common beat.
And dancing: Mimi,
a memory of desire,
doing her funky
shake and bake.
Lois rising from
her wheelchair, wanting
to slow dance again.
And the daughter
I did not have,
lingering at the side,
quiet, watching, wanting
to learn the steps.

Death at Dinner

I order the trout,
he the spare ribs. This man
I was a boy with
through college and war
asks how I think about death,
now we're in our seventies.
I don't think about it much,
I say. It's the present—
what to do, what to eat.

My friend regrets
all he'll miss. Isn't that,
I say, the human curse—
never to be satisfied,
and what's worse,
to hunger for more
so strongly we feed
ourselves a fishy story
of afterlife.

After coffee,
we rise from tufted armchairs,
murmuring of our bond,
of another departure,
of another visit, soon,
and as we step out
into air gone soggy,
into a cold, quiet rain,
without a prayer
of staying dry, I'm wishing
I'd had the poached salmon.

Night Game

On this small
planet streaking
through time and sky
—telekinesis or
a Feller fastball
to the moon—
stories, visions, lore
pass from lip
to hungry lip,
reassure the quaking
in the stands
who play their own games
of choice and chance,
luck and love, who run
their aimless course
toward an ever-
ebbing finish,
without fans,
ever hoping for
a score, before
the light's extinguished.

A Moment

I've had a son
and another
an other
a home
many homes
a love   the law
a sister   a war
a turn as star
a BB gun
an M-16
flags   brasses
losses   wins
injuries   causes
my stars
I a boy
of western skies
my dippers
stars determined
crossing
this eastern sky
my Idaho sky
Portland
those I loved
in their later time
crossing toward
my later time
I one guest of time
this moment
my stars
night sky unbroken

Notes

ao dais
often silk, the traditional dress of Vietnamese women,
which consists of a long tunic with slits on either side
and wide trousers beneath. Pronounced "ow-zeye."

APO
the Army Post Office.

The City
the one square mile of London comprised of the great financial
and commercial institutions as well as Fleet Street
and its newspaper and publishing worlds.

croup
a horse's hindquarters.

cyclo
a three-wheeled motored taxi.

debride
the surgical removal of lacerated, devitalized,
or contaminated tissue.

mermite
a container used to transport hot food.

nón lá
a palm-leaf conical hat, a symbol of the Vietnamese people.

nuoc mam
a sauce made of fish, such as anchovies, fermented in brine.

saddletree
the frame of a saddle.

skreegh
a screech or shriek.

sugarfoot
a wrestler's lead leg, more exposed to the opponent.

VC
Viet Cong, the irregular South Vietnam forces that supported
the North during the "American War."

Acknowledgments

Adanna Literary Journal: "Earline," "The Home Front"

Aethlon: "Counting Marbles"

Alaska Quarterly Review: "Sizes," selected for the
        Best American Poetry's Pick of the Week

Bellevue Literary Review: "Army Photographer,
        Research Dermatologist"

Cabin Fever: "Spooning"

Café Review: "Buddies for Life," "The Dance,"
        "Moving Day," "Walking to Another Life"

Connecticut Review: "In Country: Day One"

Porthole, Briery Creek Press, 2012, "Super Bowl III"

Chautauqua Literary Journal and *Porthole:* "Hunted"

Diode: "Portland," "Second Tie"

Hamilton Stone Review: "Chow Time"

Hollins Critic: "The Table"

I-70 Review: "Strangers"

Innisfree Poetry Journal: "Diminished"

Little Patuxent Review: "All Went Well"

Minimus: "Before Night Falls"

MiPOesias: "Lookin' Good"

New Ohio Review: "Bank Shot"

Off the Record—Poems by Lawyers: "Blind Date"

Poemeleon: "Pram"

Poet Lore: "Urgencies"

Potomac Review and *Porthole:* "The Operating Room"

Rhino: "A Moment," "The Upshot"

River Styx: "Medevac Chopper," "Treasure"

Roanoke Review: "Side by Side at the Zoo," "More,"
        "Porcelain"

Valparaiso Poetry Review: "Bitterroot," "Freight,"
        "Heart Attack," "I'm Old, I Hear Things"
        "Night Game," "Whistled Alive"

An anniversary photo of Greg and Lois taken by their son, Danny.

Bio

BORN MONTHS BEFORE the end of WWII, Greg McBride's life has been marked by the military, athletics, law, and poetry. His peripatetic childhood—he was an "Army brat"—took him to California, Texas, Arizona, Utah, Missouri, Okinawa, Oregon, Yokohama, Maryland, and Pennsylvania.

In later years, he was a Pennsylvania state wrestling champion, an Army photographer in the Vietnam War, a public service lawyer in Washington, D.C., a father, a grandfather, and a leader on behalf of the revitalization of his hometown. In his 50s, McBride began writing poems and several years later founded the *Innisfree Poetry Journal*, currently in its 19th year of biannual publication. At the age of 67, he published his first full-length collection of poems, *Porthole*, (Briery Creek Press, 2012), which won the Liam Rector First Book Prize for Poetry.

Other honors include the *Boulevard* Emerging Poet prize and grants in poetry from the Maryland State Arts Council. McBride's work has appeared in such journals as *Alaska Quarterly*, *Bellevue*, *Gettysburg Review*, *New Ohio Review*, *Rhino*, *River Styx*, and *Salmagundi*.

A Note About the Typeface

Linotype.com has the following to say about the Electra font family, used in this book for both interior and exterior, text and titles.

"Electra is an original face designed for Linotype in 1935 by William A. Dwiggins, the eminent American artist and illustrator who also created the Caledonia series. The type, which falls into the 'modern' family of type styles, is not based upon any traditional model and is not an attempt to revive or reconstruct any historic type. Because it avoids the extreme contrast of thick and thin elements that mark most modern faces, Electra provides a new 'texture' in book pages."

This book was printed in the United States of America
by Lightning Source LLC,
a business unit of the Ingram Content Group.

Book design and composition by Patric Pepper.

Also from Pond Road Press

Messages, by Piotr Gwiazda
Parts & Labor, by Gregory Hischak
Radio in the Basement, by Bernard Jankowski
Familiar at First, Then Strange, by Meredith Holmes
Shubad's Crown, by Meredith Holmes (out of print)
Blue Morning Light, by David Salner
Human Animal, by Anne Becker
Crooked Speech, by Sid Gold
Tough Heaven: Poems of Pittsburgh, by Jack Gilbert
(out of print)
Walking the Sunken Boards, by Linda Blaskey,
Gail Braune Comorat,Wendy Elizabeth Ingersoll
and Jane C. Miller
Season of Harvest, by Linda Blaskey & jim bourey

Available from online retail booksellers,
the Ingram Content Group (wholesale orders)
and through Pond Road Press.

pondroadpress@hotmail.com

www.ingramcontent.com/pod-product-compliance
Lightning Source LLC
Chambersburg PA
CBHW020211090426
42734CB00008B/1024